M000249962

SUPERBASE 21

BARKSDALE

SUPERBASE 21
BARKSDALE
Home of the Mighty Eighth
David Davies & Mike Vines

OSPREY
AEROSPACE

Acknowledgements

Photographs were taken on Nikon, large format Pentax and Hasselblad equipment and the film used was exclusively Fuji 100ASA and Fuji Velvia. Thanks go to Trevor Drake, John Cohen and Graham Rutherford of Fuji Professional Film Division. To Alan Dunn of Dunn's Photographic Laboratories for superb processing of all the transparencies, and to Phil Goldsmith, branch manager of KJ&P, Birmingham, for the loan of equipment.

Published in 1991 by Osprey Publishing Limited
59 Grosvenor Street, London W1X 9DA

© David Davies and Mike Vines 1991

All rights reserved. Apart from any fair dealing for the purpose of private study, research, criticism or review, as permitted under the Copyright, Designs and Patents Act, 1988, no part of the publication may be reproduced, stored in a retrieval system, or transmitted in any form or by any means, electronic, electrical, chemical, mechanical, optical, photocopying, recording or otherwise, without prior written permission. All enquiries should be addressed to the Publishers.

British Library Cataloguing in Publication Data

Davies, David 1943–
    Barksdale.—(Superbase v.21)
    1. United States. Air bases
    I. Title   II. Vines, Mike   III. Series
    358.4170473

ISBN 1 85532 137 8

Editor Tony Holmes
Page design Paul Kime
Printed in Hong Kong

Front cover Departing Barksdale's 11,756 ft runway is *Miss Fitt II* (B-52G 58-0238), off on a training sortie before coming back to the circuit for a session of touch and goes. The quadricycle undercarriage has just started to swivel during the retraction process and the outrigger wheels just inboard of the auxiliary fuel tanks are folding flat into the underside of the wing

Back cover With the large intakes of its two 9065 lb thrust General Electric TF34-GE100 turbofans silhouetted against the sky, and refuelling receptacle open, *Blade 21* starts to move into position to receive fuel from the KC-135A tanker

Title page Plugged in and drinking fast. B-52G Stratofortress, call-sign *Doom 64*, holds a steady position beneath the KC-135A

Right 83-0075, a white-top KC-10A of the 2nd BW, receives its 'roll-on' palletized forward passenger seating. In the background is 84-0188. Its dark scheme will become the norm as operational requirements dictate an increasing need for better camouflage. Only a few KC-10As will continue to operate with the traditional white and grey colour scheme

For a catalogue of all books published by Osprey Aerospace please write to:

The Marketing Manager, Consumer Catalogue Department Osprey Publishing Ltd, 59 Grosvenor Street, London, W1X 9DA

Introduction

We're in the deep south of the United States, it's hot enough to fry eggs on your camera body and the humidity is through the roof. In north west Louisiana, just off Interstate 20 at Bossier City (pronounced Bozcher) you might be lucky enough to see the sky darkened by an aluminium overcast – the B-52s are coming home to Barksdale.

This is bomber country and the 2nd Bombardment Wing operates more than 30 B-52Gs. They share Barksdale's huge 15/33 runway with A-10A Thunderbolt IIs of the 917th Tactical Fighter Wing, the largest TFW in the Air Force Reserve, their own KC-10A Extender and KC-135 tanker force, plus various training types like the T-37B Tweet, T-38 Talon and the C-21A Learjet. Add to this a variety of interesting visitors from the US Navy and Marine Corps and you've got a circuit that's never dull.

With a total of almost 75 heavies on base, the 2nd BW has nearly twice as many aircraft as any other bomb wing, over 30 per cent of these machines being on 24-hours a day ground alert. To enable them to be deployed at very short notice, the crews of both the B-52s and the tanker force stay on base in special quarters for seven days at a time. The over used word 'awesome' takes on a whole new meaning when applied to these bombers. They are configured with six Air Launched Cruise Missiles (ALCM) under each wing and a possible eight more on a rotary launcher in the bomb bay.

Barksdale is the headquarters of the 8th Air Force which is responsible for the operation and training of all SAC forces in the eastern half of the United States, Europe and the Middle East. Back in World War 2 it is estimated that 350,000 Americans served in the 8th AF when it was based in England and commanded by Brig General Ira C Eaker. The 8th AF at its peak would put up more than 2000 four-engined bombers and over a 1000 fighters on a single mission. It became known as the 'Mighty Eighth,' a title which they are justifiably proud of today.

So the transport's waiting. Slam on your hat and let's go see the world of the 'Mighty Eighth'. Just a word of warning: US bases don't welcome unannounced visitors and sightseeing trips are mostly impossible to arrange. The 8th AF museum is however open to the public and visitors are welcome. Our thanks to the public affairs office at Barksdale for arranging our visit, in particular to Sgt Stephen Pierce; also to Tech Sgt Larry McLean and museum curator Buck Rigg.

Right The 917th Consolidated Aircraft Maintenance Squadron (CAMS) are proud of their bombing-up role, an operation where speed and safety are of the essence. On their hangar wall is a 'jammer' trolley, manned by an 'incredible hulk' that you certainly wouldn't want to meet on a dark night. This trolley is used to jam the bombs and missiles onto the A-10's underwing hardpoints

Contents

Barksdale BUFFs

Right As the sun sinks in the west BUFF 0238 throws a large shadow on the Barksdale runway approach. Behind the cockpit is a low visibility SAC shield, whilst beneath the nose the right eyeball of the Electro-Optical Viewing System (EVS) has been rotated to show the infra-red scanner window. Clearly visible at the wing root is the Strakelet, a fillet which serves to identify Air Launched Cruise Missile (ALCM) carriers, as agreed upon by both the USA and the USSR during the Strategic Arms Limitation Talks (SALT)

Below Line astern of the tanker, *Sagittarius II*, topped with JP4, is cleared to leave the refuelling area and pops its roll control spoiler panel atop the right wing to continue its training mission

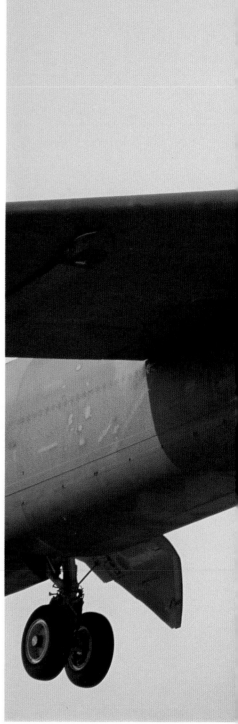

Above The second customer for fuel on this sortie is *Doom 65*, a B-52G nicknamed *Equapoise II*, and it is seen here filling the boomer's window. It's a slow and careful business edging 185 feet of wing and more than 160 feet of fuselage up to the back of the tanker

Right The KC-135's high speed boom hangs out on its V-wings as the pilot of *Equapoise II* inches forward on the throttles

Opposite Contact. As the boom passes over the bomber's cockpit the crew lose sight of it and from then on it's down to the boomer to fly it into the air refuelling receptacle further back along the fuselage. Stratofortress crews are required to keep current with air-to-air refuelling on a monthly basis

Above Throttles wide open on all eight Pratt & Whitney J57 turbojets, this B-52G leaves a wake of black smoke as it overshoots the approach to runway 33. The first B-52, a B-model, was delivered to SAC 35 years ago, the then new jet bomber replacing the Convair B-36 in frontline service. In the early 1960s there were more than 600 B-52s active with SAC, but now only the G and H models remain in service, their number totalling around 260 aircraft

Right B-52G, 58-0238, roars overhead with its single slotted fowler-type flaps still fully extended

Below It's time to get out of the way when you see the tell-tale smoke from the Pratt & Whitney J57-P-43WB turbojets. Two of Barksdale's BUFFs let it all hang out as they prepare to recover back at base. Circuit crunching is a part of everyday life for the 2nd BW, and more often then not the whole crew goes along for the ride

Right 58-0238, nicknamed *Miss Fit II*, makes an approach over the VIsual Approach Slope Indicator (VASI) lights. The unblinkered device under the nose of the BUFF is a Hughes AN/AAQ-6 Forward Looking Infra Red (FLIR) unit

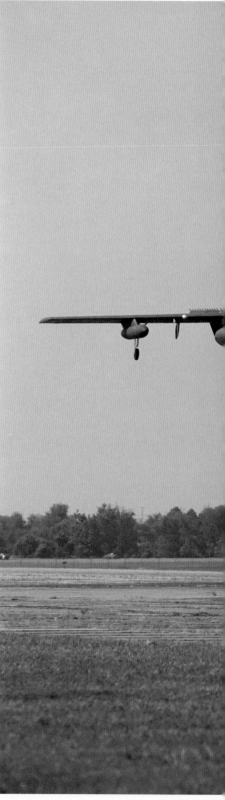

Right *Miss Fit II* is now only a split second away from a perfect touchdown. The wing/fuselage junction contouring identifies this B-52G as a cruise missile carrier

Above 58-0238 comes back to the steamy heat of Barksdale's runway 33. The small white protuberance on top of the rear fuselage is the ALQ-117 retractable aerial

Left The VASI lights can be seen glowing red through the shimmering heat of eight engine exhausts as 58-0238 heads for a perfect touchdown. Although the lights are showing red from ground level, the pilot, if he is at the correct angle of approach, will see red lights above white. If he is too high, they're all white, too low all red. The roll control spoilers, here deployed on the starboard wing, are crucial aids for the pilot during crosswind recoveries

Above About ten feet to go as the 10,000 foot marker board comes up

Below A wisp of smoke indicates that the rear bogie has kissed the surface of the runway a fraction of a second ahead of the front wheels

Left This 2nd BW pilot gets all four wheels in contact with runway 33 at the same time, hence the smoke. The quadricycle undercarriage has a cross-wing landing facility which allows the wheels to be pointed at an angle of up to 20 degrees off centre of the fuselage. The BUFF crew can then swivel the bomber into the wind, the aircraft's undercarriage staying firmly aligned with the runway

Overleaf While other B-52s soak up the sun on Barksdale's ramp, the rear BUFF slowly threads its way through over two dozen bombers on its way to the runway. The 2nd BW has been resident in Louisiana since April 1 1963, and comprises the 62nd and 596th Bomber Squadrons. Crews of the 62nd BS perform the conventional bombing role, whilst the 596th operate B-52Gs modified for ALCM nuclear strikes

Above The B-52G was introduced into service in 1959 and has been subjected to several major equipment updates since that date. Radars, weapons control systems, navigation systems and display units have all been vastly improved, increasing the BUFF's capability and survivability. Here, *The Witch II* exposes some of its black boxes for minor maintenance

Right Airman Alan Fulgham and Airwoman Toni Carter, both of the 2nd Operational Maintenance Squadron, check over the EVS before moving on to the updated electronics hidden under the nose radome

Left An 'alert' aircraft commander and co-pilot from the 596th BS leave their special quarters to demonstrate crew positions in the B-52. As can be seen, there's plenty of glass and a real 'fist full of throttles!'

Above Facing forward on the lower deck is the crew station for the navigator and radar navigator/bombardier, otherwise known as the 'blackhole'. The inhabitants of this 'office' both sit on downward-firing ejection seats

Above An officer from the 596th BS wears his *Excalibur* arm patch with pride. Strategic Air Command's motto, *Peace is our profession*, has changed recently to *War is our profession, Peace is our product*

Left World War 2 nose art is reincarnated on Stratofortress 92590, the original *Better Duck* being a B-17 Fortress of the 95th Bomb Group

Opposite *Equipoise II*, just back from a training mission which included air-to-air refuelling, patiently awaits the attention of the 2nd OMS

Right 'Don't mess with a striking cobra when the dice are loaded against you'. That's the message coming across loud and clear from this *Snake Eyes* nose art on B-52G 57-6504

Below The nose art on this B-52G (57-6520) is dedicated to B-24 Liberator 272786, which, as part of the 31st Bomb Squadron of the 5th Bomb Group, 13th AF, completed 35 combat missions in the Pacific theatre during World War 2

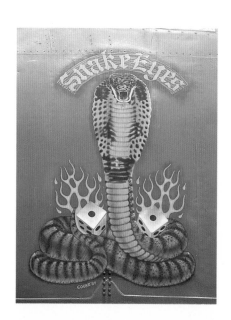

Above This *PETIE 3rd* nose art on 58-0177 is dedicated to General John C Meyer, Commander-in-Chief of SAC from May 1972 to July 1974. He scored 26 victories in *PETIE 2nd*, a P-51D (41-4151) assigned to the 487th FS of the 352nd Fighter Group, based at Bodney in England, during World War 2

Above right 57-6509, alias *Nine O Nine II*, is dedicated to World War 2 B-17, 42-31909 of the 91st Bomb Group (BG)

Below right 58-0233 *Chow Hound #2* commemorates B-17 42-31367 of the 91st BG, 8th AF. This particular Fortress was lost on 8 August 1944

Above The waveguide antennae are clearly visible beneath the female archer on the nose of 58-0252, otherwise known as *Sagittarius II*

Left 58-0185 is nick named *El Lobo II* after its World War 2 counterpart. Beneath the right wing is an ALCM pylon, whilst the 'warts' under the nose house Hughes AN/AAQ-6 FLIR (left) and the Westinghouse AN/AVQ-22 Steerable TV System (STV) (right)

Left *Miss Fit II* simmers in temperatures of 100°F. The fairing beneath the nose art houses the ALQ-117 radar warning antenna

Below Keep sharp boys! It sure is a heck of a job being the top team representing the 2nd BW from Barksdale. Before loading the ALCMs, Tech Sgt Terry P Hearn checks to make sure that Staff Sgt Barrs, Sgt Ronald L Luvisi Jr, Staff Sgt Richard J Hanke and Staff Sgt Glenn D Keppler are not wearing any rings and watches which could cause FOD (foreign object damage). These guys, all attached to the 2nd MMS (Munitions Maintenance Squadron), were the winning team at the *Giant Sword* SAC weapons loading competition at Fairchild AFB in September 1989. They are pictured practising for the 1990 competition, an event which had to be cancelled soon after this photograph was taken owing to the US involvement in *Operation Desert Shield* in Saudi Arabia

Overleaf When moving the ALCM cradle with the ground electronics unit the pylon has to be lined up accurately beneath the aircraft's weapons hardpoint. The missiles, six on each cradle, are already mounted on their own pylon. The crouching team member under the wing is in typical stance – back bent. The team are trained to adopt this position when arming the aircraft so that they don't injure themselves. They walk or run like this for up to an hour non-stop – this is how long it can take to complete the loading, although they would not regard this as a winning time

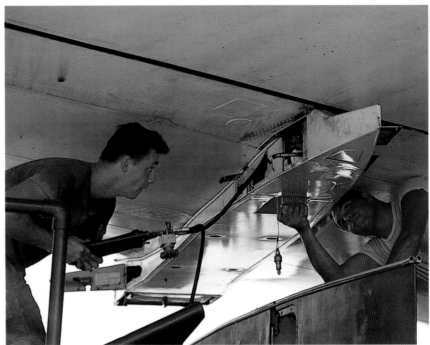

Above Staff Sgt Keppler (left), with sweat dripping off his chin, pumps in grease to the underwing hardpoint, while Staff Sgt Barrs monitors his progress. This operation has to be carried out before the ALCMs can be hoisted from their cradle

Left In this shot, taken from the rear of the ALCM cradle, you can see the folded fins of the dummy AGM-86B cruise missiles

Left 'Always protect your butt' takes on a whole new meaning when you look at the BUFF's rear. From this angle the complexities of the 'old bird's' tail feathers are clearly visible. The fairing (top left) houses the ECM package, whilst the radome above the four 0.5 in (12.7 mm) machine guns houses the AN/ASG-15 search radar

Above This B-52G dominates the scene on Barksdale's enormous ramp. Dwarfed in the background are six T-37Bs

Left Four of the BUFF's Pratt & Whitney J57-P-43WB turbojets exposed for engine checks

Above It's nearly midnight but phased maintenance goes on around the clock. The men of the 2nd Organizational Maintenance Squadron (OMS) work on 57-6509 (*Nine-O-NIne II*), whilst in the foreground 59-2580 (*Sheriff's Posse No 2*) awaits attention

It's dawn, the coolest time on the ramp, and the KC-10A's navigation lights start to blink, ready for another day's flying. In the foreground a BUFF has arrived back after a 10-hour night training sortie

What a great sight – eight of Barksdale's 30-plus B-52Gs mark time on the ramp. In the background are around 30 A-10As of the 917th Tactical Fighter Wing (TFW), Air Force Reserve (AFRES)

It's 5.45 am and we're in for another beautiful deep south sunrise. The sound of the crickets' steady beat is broken by the man-made rumbling of J-57s starting up, the B-52 force limbering up for another day's flying

'KC and the SAC band'

The heat haze adds to the sizzling temperatures on the ramp as KC-10As of the 2nd BW/32nd ARS mingle their exhaust gasses with those of the B-52s'

Above Frequent liquid intake is the order of the day at Barksdale. Here the ground crew of KC-10A 83-0075, nicknamed *International Express*, take a break in the shadow of the freight door

Left KC-10A Extender, B-52Gs, a taxying KC-135A, a C-21A and at the top, the 'alert' B-52Gs armed with 12 ALCMs under the wings. These aircraft have their own specially guarded ramp and this is as near as we were allowed to get to it! Ever wished for a 10,000 mm lens?

Below With its refuelling boom in the lowered position for maintenance, KC-10A 79-1710 of the 2nd BW receives attention to its centre engine. When an aircraft is over 58 feet high a cherry-picker comes in handy when it's time to 'check the oil'. Barksdale's distinctive fleur-de-lis symbol stands out on the tail

Right A white-top KC-10A looms out of the early morning sky

Above Sunrise, and the ground crew are preparing a dripping wet KC-10A for flight. You can just see the 8th AF Museum's KC-97L in the mist between the wheels of this giant tanker

Right The dawn breaks to find maintenance personnel already hard at work preparing aircraft for the first flights of the day

Right The weak morning light floods three white-top KC-10As. As the KC-10s pass through their major service overhauls many are being resprayed in matt grey

Above Seen from the air-conditioned comfort of a KC-135A flight deck, a pair of KC-10A Extenders bake at the base of Barksdale's tower. Both the 2nd and the 32nd Air Refuelling Squadrons (ARS) are attached to the 2nd BW

Left Low-visibility decals are applied to Extender 84-0188 *Touch of Class/Nulli Secondus* (Second to None)

Above left Sharing the ramp with *Touch of Class* is KC-10A 85-0028, an aircraft which has Wing badges but no nose art

Above right The distinctive badge of the 2nd ARS

Previous pages Whilst other squadron aircraft are aloft performing tanking tasks, Extender 91710 receives attention to its refuelling boom. The 'red carpet' painted across the ramp leads to the host building for SAC's Bombing and Navigation Symposium, an event which brings together the Command's finest crews

Right SAC ordered 60 KC-10A Extenders In December 1977 the first aircraft reaching the 32nd ARS at Barksdale in March 1981

Above When you're chauffeuring in a CDV (Colonel's Distinguished Visitor), you have to make sure you stop right by the red carpet painted on the ramp

Above Three General Electric CF6-50C2 turbofan engines pull the
KC-10 skywards

Right Based on the DC-10-30CF convertible freighter airliner, the Extender
required many modifications for military use. One of the major changes centred
around the installation of seven bladder fuel cells in the lower fuselage
compartments, this mod allowing the KC-10 to carry an extra 15,000 gallons
of fuel

The 2nd BW operates 19 KC-10As in support of its B-52s

Clear of the runway, the initial rate of climb for the Extender is almost 3000 feet per minute

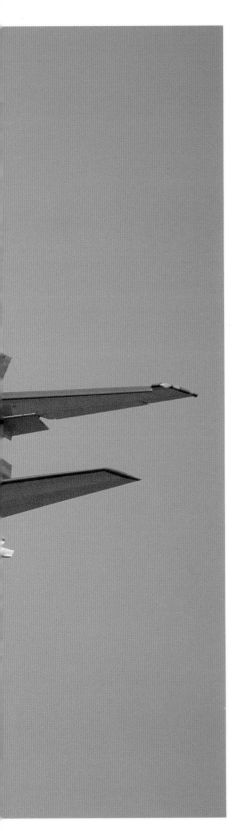

Above A KC-10A with gear retracted and flaps travelling just after take-off

Left A map of Louisiana state is painted near the nose of this Extender

Below Under the tailplane is the advanced aerial refuelling boom, controlled by a digital fly-by-wire system. Unlike the KC-135, it's armchair comfort for the boomer in the KC-10A

Right Looking good for a textbook recovery, a KC-10 closes on Barksdale's runway 15

Overleaf At work in the office. Aircraft commander Captain Tamra Rank and instructor pilot Captain Sue Des Jardins share a smile with flight engineer T/Sgt Brian Kelly and boomer S/Sgt Lynn Stoddard on the flight deck of the roomy KC-10A

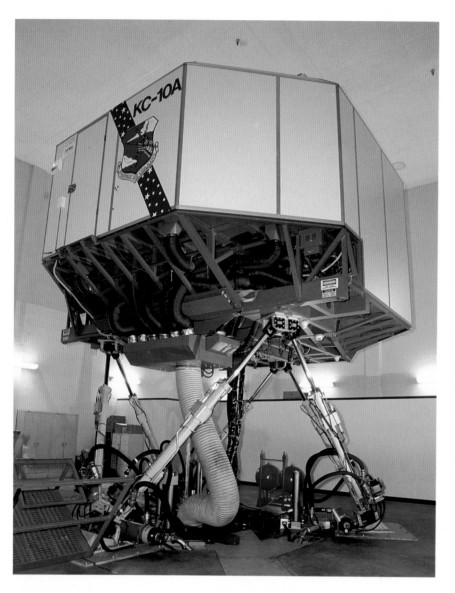

Above A fairly innocuous looking piece of equipment on the outside, this Link-Miles KC-10A simulator is where crews sweat it out practising emergency procedures for several hours at a time. Usually, the simulator is occupied for 16 hours a day

Right Shooting an approach at night in the KC-135A simulator, Captain Bryan Browning and 1st Lt Dennis Thornton practice emergency procedures

Veteran
refuellers

Boeing KC-135A 60-0316 of the 71st
ARS, based at Barksdale, is just about
to clean up after take-off

Above As the band plays 'Up into the Wild Blue Yonder', Colonel Allen, Chief-of-Staff 8th AF, welcomes his distinguished visitors who have arrived in 60-0355, a KC-135A from Wurtsmith AFB, Michigan. The musicians are from Barksdale's resident 745th AF band squadron. Their duties include on-base ceremonial and troop morale functions, and off-base support of Air Force recruiting and community relations events

Right Barksdale's black asphalt runway rolls out ahead of the 71st ARS KC-135A as it starts its protracted take-off. Part of the 2nd BW, the 71ARS flies the old A-model KC-135

Right Known as *Smokey Joe*, the KC-135A Stratotanker first entered service with SAC in 1957

Above Four Pratt & Whitney J57 turbojets haul this KC-135A away from Barksdale. Additional fuel for refuelling missions is carried in bladder cells beneath the cabin floor, leaving the cabin clear for cargo and troops

Left Lt Col Gary Love reaches across to check the throttles

Above Co-pilot 1st Lt Dennis Thornton holds the well worn control column during a left turn on to the refuelling track

Previous pages Aboard KC-135A 63-7982 of the 71st ARS. The aircraft is being flown by Lt Col Gary Love and co-pilot 1st Lt Dennis Thornton

Above While the aircraft commander turns the Stratotanker around for another refuelling track, the co-pilot glances at his note card before changing radio frequencies

Right Aircraft commander, co-pilot and navigator get busy as they leave the refuelling area to practice a timed arrival over a map point without the use of modern navigational aids

Above left Navigator Capt John Brislan (of Welsh ancestry, perhaps) works with the charts to get the KC-135A over the target right on the button

Above right Boomer, Airman 1st Class Rodney Smith, shoots a sun fix through the roof of the Stratotanker

Right All KC-135s with the 2nd BW are A-models, but some are painted grey whilst others have been camouflaged

Louisiana 'Hogs

78-0657 comes up from the ranges for some fuel. The blue and gold fin stripes mark this A-10A, call sign *Blade 21*, as a 46th Tactical Fighter training squadron (TFTS) aircraft, attached to C Flight at Barksdale. Beneath the starboard wing is a TGM-65 Maverick training round

78-0657 backs-off to show a clean
aeroplane for photography before
returning to Barksdale

Above Not too far to go now. The A-10 is an excellent platform for aerial refuelling due to its docile handling characteristics and capacious canopy

Right In the slot, *Blade 22* gets a drink. The 30 mm General Electric GAU-8A Avenger multi-barrel cannon (the weapon which the aeroplane was designed around) is well lit at this angle. Also visible on the port side of the nose is a Pave Penny laser receiver and tracking pod. It detects and tracks designated targets 'illuminated' by a friendly laser operated either by troops in the field, or by other aircraft. The Pave Penny feeds data into the pilot's Head Up Display (HUD) whilst simultaneously updating and directing the seeker head on the Maverick missile

Previous pages Lined up ready for action over the bombing ranges, nine Warthogs of the 46th TFTS await their AFRES drivers

Above Just back from the bombing range, a 47th TFS (green fin top) Thunderbolt II kisses the runway

Right Awaiting their turn are A-10As of the 46th TFTS, C Flight (blue fin top/gold band)

Left Climbing into a hot cockpit, this pilot is about to head out to the local range to expend his war load of small practice bombs on ground targets

Above Awaiting its turn to run in on the weapons range, this A-10A (76-0552) is equipped with a red-capped Pave Penny laser receiver and tracking pod

Trusty trainers

Right 71st Flying Training Wing Cessna T-37B Tweets await their pilots on the vast Barksdale pan. Part of the Accelerated-Co-Pilot Enrichment Programme, these veteran trainers are used by younger SAC right-seaters to build up their flying hours

Below Canopy cranked open, the roomy cockpit of the T-37 invites the pilot to jump in and take the little jet aloft

Above Thorough pre-flight checks are completed before the Tweet crew head off into the maze of taxy tracks that cover Barksdale

Right A 2nd BW co-pilot waves off for the runway in something lighter than his usual B-52

Above 67-22253, a T-37B Tweet of No 2 Flt, 8th FTS, is based at Barksdale but is part of the 71st Flying Training Wing (FTW) from Vance AFB, Oklahoma

Left The crew of Tweet 57-2313 get the thumbs-up from the ramp marshal. The ear defenders are vital as the high-pitched squeal generated by the two Continental J69-T-25 turbojets is the nearest thing to white noise. The '1' on the fin depicts an aircraft from No 1 Flt, 8th FTS/71st FTW, from Vance AFB. There are T-37Bs from Nos 1, 2 and 3 Flts in this view

Right 68-8193, a Vance AFB T-38A of the 71st FTW, gets ready to go

Above The crew of 68-8193 complete strapping-in before start-up

Above Looking like the 'right stuff', two pilots from the 90th FTS/80th TFW taxy to the ramp after a training sortie in their Talon

Right The stylized *EURO-NATO* fin emblem marks this T-38A Talon as belonging to the 90 TFS/80th FTW, normally based at Sheppard AFB, Texas. Besides training raw recruits for the USAF, the 80th FTW also instructs European pilots from NATO member countries

Far right C-21A Learjets of Det 3, 1401st Military Airlift Squadron, based at Barksdale. Five of these 'flying limousines' make up the detachment

Transient ramp

Right Split wing tip airbrakes deployed, this Grumman EA-6B Prowler from reservist-manned VAQ-309 'Axemen' settles on to the runway at Barksdale. These electronic countermeasure four-seaters (a pilot and three electronic warfare officers) provide a protective screen around the fleet, ride shotgun for strike formations and gather electronic intelligence for the US Navy

Below A towering B-52G dwarfs a Marines F/A-18A Hornet of VMFA-115 'Silver Eagles' as it leaves the ramp after a short stay on base

Out and about

Left Attending the antenna end of runway 15, and nonchalant to the goings on behind them, is S/Sgt Larry McLean and Sgt Deana Cramer, both atttached to the 46th Comms Group. The B-52G in the background is completing a 'wet' take-off

Overleaf Inside the 8th AF Command Post, the 20 ft high display status screens are set up with sanitized material for our cameras. But even from this you can get an idea of the kind of information it usually contains – ICBM daily alert status, aircraft alert status and world weather. The 'Mighty Eighth' is a vital link in SACs mission to deter war. It can respond to a variety of threats with its mixed force of 46 B-1Bs, 160 B-52Gs and several TR-1 and RC-135 recce aircraft. This impressive fleet is supported by 295 frontline KC-135s (plus 80 KC-135s of the ANG and AFRES) and 35 KC-10A Extenders. SAC usually maintains up to 30 per cent of its bomber and tanker force on 24-hour ground alert. The Eighth is also responsible for a single Minuteman II (ICBM) Wing at Whiteman AFB, MO

		TYPE	MSN	DEPART	DE
021443	BARKSDL	1	KC-135	HHD	
021525	LORING	1	KC-135	HHD	GRIFFIS	TO
022134	GRISSOM	1	KC-135	ETTF	LORING	FAR
022346	EAKER	2	B-52G	RFLAG	LORING	FARP
	EAKER				NELLI

SIOP COMMITTED SORTIE	XXX		XX	XXX	XXX	XXX
SIOP REQUIRED ALERT	XXX	XX	XX	XXX	XXX	XX
OFF ALERT	XXX	X	X	XX	XXX	XXX
TOTAL ON ALERT				XX	XX	XXX
HOME GND ALERT	XXX	X	XX			
DISPERSED GND ALERT	XXX	X	X	XX	XX	
G/LANCE ABN ALERT				XX	XX	
PC AIRBORNE					XXX	

R/S-400

LAST PAGE 1

UNCLASSIFIED

ICBM DAILY ALERT STATUS

BASE	SIOP A CAT OFF ON	A CAT OFF ON GRF	A CAT OFF ON	TOTAL ON
ELSWRH	XXX			
GRNDF	XXX	XXX	8AF	
WHITM	XXX	XXX		
		XXX	XX	
MINOT		X		XXX
MALSTM	XXX		XX	XXX
WARRE	XXX	XXX	15AF	XXX
	XXX	X	XX	XXX
TOTAL	XXX	XXX	X	XXX
	XXX		XX	XXX
	XXX	XX		XXX
			XX	XXX
				XXX
				XXX

R/S-400

UNCLASSIFIED

LAST PAGE 1

HOLD

UNCLASSIFIED &AFEURO

					AS OF 19 JUN 1756Z		
		MX	ITEM	DEN PT	WIND	X IND	REMARKS
	64	37	280/12		977	BLU NOSIG
	61	45	220/04		83	CIGE03S
	61	48	240/05		83	974 CAVOK NOSIG
			230/14		82	CIGE03B VIB
			300/16028	21	893	GLU
						CIGE05B

UNCLASSIFIED

PAGE 01

Left Keeping a sharp eye on the Barksdale circuit and ramp is Sgt Mark Green, with help from Airmen Bart Moon, Johnathon Cain, John Houston and T/Sgt Lynda Jaspers. In this view of the ramp 13 B-52Gs and over 40 A-10s can be seen

Above No funny business is tolerated by these guys! Guards from the Security Police Squadron show off their *Peacekeeper* armoured personnel carrier, complete with mounted M60 machine gun, in front of an alert status KC-135A of the 71st ARS

Vintage SAC

Left Boeing B-47E Stratojet 32276 was last used by the Atomic Testing Centre in New Mexico. In 1970 it arrived to start the Eighth AF Museum's collection. It is painted up to represent a B-47 used by the 2nd BW at Hunter AFB in Georgia back in the 1950s

Below Also to be seen in the museum is this B-17G Flying Fortress, serialled 338289. *Yankee Doodle II* is painted up to represent an aircraft used by the 303rd Bombardment Group. Better known as the *Hells Angels*, the 303rd was one of the top B-17 outfits in the Army Air Force during World War 2

Left above This Boeing KC-97L was last operated by the Utah ANG. It is not on public show yet and before putting it on display, Mr Buck Rigg, curator of the Museum, hopes to re-convert it to G-model specs to represent an aircraft operated by the 2nd AREFW, 2nd BW, when they were based in Georgia. The museum's outside area is to be doubled in size to accommodate this and the other large aircraft that are still to be moved across from the east side of the base

Left below Veteran F-4C Phantom II 63-7532 is now the 47th Tactical Fighter Squadron's mascot

Above Stored awaiting future display are a pair of North American AGM-28 Hound Dog missiles once carried in twos by the Stratofortress. This 43 foot long weapon (the large nose cones are just out of the picture) was withdrawn from the SAC inventory in 1976 – at its peak there were over 600 missiles on hand to equip 29 B-52G/H squadrons. Powered by an underslung P&W J52 turbojet, it could cruise at up to Mach 2.1 and, if need be, the missile's jet power could be used to boost the B-52's take-off performance, the Hound Dog's 'gas tank' being topped up from the bomber's own internal fuel supply once the aircraft was airborne

Left The diminutive decoy missile, the McDonnell ADM-20 Quail, served with SAC between 1960 and 1978. Powered by a GE J85 turbojet, two of these 13 foot-long missiles could be released from the bomb bay of a B-52 and mimic the aircraft's speed and height. The trick aspect of the Quail, however, centred around its ability to paint a B-52-size blip on an enemy radar screen!

Below Acquired from General Dynamics, this engineering mock-up is the nearest the Museum can get to an F-111 at the moment. When extra space for museum exhibits becomes available at Barksdale this test frame will be finished off and displayed as a standard F-111 'Aardvark'